575-365:
Haiku Every Day

Ginger L Franklin PhD

575-365: Haiku Every Day
Author: Ginger L Franklin PhD

Copyright © 2022 Ginger L Franklin PhD. All Rights Reserved.
Published by Ginger L Franklin PhD.

ISBN 978-1-6781-8026-3

No introduction
Enjoy reading my poems
No refunds issued

As the lily slept
She dreamed of the coming rain
But she did not wake

Your voice is magic
Bringing transcendence to us
The spell of the soul

What does pegal mean?
You crazy, lovesick, weird-o
This coin has two sides

You float around, ghost
Impenetrable fortress
Of mysteries kept

I heard you singing
Time passed and you held my hand
I saw you sleeping

Matsuri taiko
Odaiko, chu, okedo
Calls the thunder forth

Cactus wren sings low
Dust across the plains haunts us
Yet this is our earth

Takoyaki line
Where does it end and where's mine?
Once a year, I wait

How long is your hair?
Knotted and hidden, it calls
Like a Geisha's neck

You can't be afraid
Your bed is against the wall
The ghost and the boy

I will bring you sweets
If you keep me in your arms
The prashad of love

I want to go home
Yet I gave it all away
I'll wander cold nights

Where are you sleeping?
Others come and go, Vshnu
You remain constant

Page fifteen is blank
Can't think of any haiku
Impossible task

The old ghost sets off
Rails through the barren desert
Steel on steel, souls meet

Kabuki mask fades
The old theatre lights dim
Actor, where's your core?

Volleyball at night
Under the Khanda and heat
Waheguru! Spike!

The serpentine Lord
Bhujanagabhushana
Wrap around my heart

I was created
Adorned by the light of truth
I was created

Don't open your eyes
How long can you hold your breath?
The specter comes near

We sing day and night
Still, our hearts cannot find you
Our words but ashes

Silent requiem
Ghosts scream into a vacuum
Laughter dissipates

Lord Shiva greets me
Open palms and silent eyes
Fragrance of lotus

In Devil's Canyon
Yogis abscond with our cash
The bug bites are free

The poodle barks shrill
She needs her kibble and pets
The soul of a wolf

In the kitchen, Love
In the dining hall, Friendship
The Langar of God

God, look upon me
Without your thoughts, I vanish
In stillness, we meet

By God's graceful glance
Awake to the Eternal
Truth gives us each breath

Sing of Ek Onkar
His name's the nectar of truth
Dripping to our tongues

As the ocean swells
So my need for you takes me
In you, I dissolve

Grandfather, you're here
Grandmother's looking for us
The ancestors call

Seeing swarms of gnats
Pretending that they are snow
I dream in this heat

The sun and the moon
Always rising and falling
Observe our spirit

Blue sky thunder cracks
Our taiko shakes the hard ground
Aozora plays

I don't fit in here
My clothes are not white enough
Or my skin, too white

Who can survive here
The learned and the hearty
Others wilt in fire

Each year, we arrive
Costumes, taiko, Sensei's fire
Generations learn

The wind blows through trees
The dust rolls in spirit clouds
Desert cleansed by rage

Ghosts, peppers, dust, rope
These are the things that live here
In silver and bone

The Pad Thai vendor
Fish, grilled squid, spice, and cold Chang
We sit under tarps

Cover your hair, child
The sun is hot and leering
You will get burned up

The empty hotel
By night, ghosts lurk in shadows
The long stay of death

Breathe is an honor
When all creation is still
Heartbeats are thunder

Green leaves fall heavy
From the tree with deepest roots
Its cast is timeless

In-between silence
Your voice is the only thing
That fills empty space

Why do you deny
That the goddess inside you
Eats death and breathes fire?

The hound's teeth tear flesh
A roar is heard through the snow
Hunting cold mountains

My loving kindness
Churns like the turbulent sea
Your boat stays anchored

The lights shine on us
The flames guide us home to you
The lights shine through us

Whirling dervish come,
Dance in the halls of Allah
His heartbeat your drum

The date palm blooms sweet
In the desert's searing heat
So my love blooms fruit

I have climbed so high
I saw the glory and light
How was it a dream?

You mock me, my God
I did all that I should have
Yet I am in Hell

Candle flames flicker
Yet your light never wavers
Burn away our guise

What a joke this life
A constant struggle for what?
Lessons from cruel Gods

Siva, why leave me?
I'm only a lonely girl.
Can I eat your soul?

The great circling
Specters' journey through ether
Clouds the sun and moon.

Chant WaheGuru
See the light shining inside
Our kitchen feeds all

Vasuki round thrice
My spine enshrined in fine silks
Your black moon embrace

The gopis tire out
Yet with his flute's finest tunes
All work, they endure

Ganesha loves sweets
The kind, blessed soul of God's son
Why not have it all?

So lazy right now
Just ten more minutes of sleep
Under the blankets

At the great Gandhi's
Funeral pyre we there wept
We all cried, "My God."

Dear God, please help me
I don't want to be nothing
Where do I go now?

I love you, Ganesh
You are our eternal gate
Where shall we go now?

The bodhisattva
Descends to this earth with love
How shall he depart?

You don't have to do
Anything, you must only be
Earth spins by itself

As water bubbles
So we inhale and exhale
Life's flow eternal

Divine words like sand
So many I can't hold you
My ink sifts away

Whisky sour night
Cold wind and dirt in my teeth
Caked with earth, I lie

Tabla skin stretched tight
Beats march and dance through the night
Procession of God

Metatron come now
We need to write together
Share your divine ink

Prayer flags wave forth
Carrying their sacred words
Old strings in the breeze

The shrine on the hill
Under the old cherry trees
Ghosts carry water

In old medinas
Mingle blood, fruit, life, and cash
Cats search for a deal

A donkey brays out
The coppersmith hammers on
Whips crack from all sides

Brew the coffee black
As night slips into the light
I can't work alone

The river, the drip
The ocean and the fine mist
The fire can't subsist

The girl and her horse
The rain through the wind and sky
Unhalting and calm

Cold breaking the day
When the old raven departs
Thunder on wings cracks

A walk through the night
The scorpion's final touch
Bare feet on hot sand

Sheets twisted and wet
The ghost and the observer
Tangled in struggle

You appear to me
Impenetrable fortress
Of love's mystery

She designs textiles
On the computer upstairs
She won't use the loom

Time to write haiku
I do not know what to do
Can't all be winners

You stood against winds
Abode of crumbling earth
You return to God

Make it a double
Toss back the liquid disease
Just leave the bottle

A whole lifetime passed
In one afternoon, we met
Our fate knew better

Seasoning on bread
Spirits gather in silence
Break and pass stale life

Dust, ghosts, and cold wind
Making the fire burn higher
The embers float on

*April Fools
Your voice is just like a magical thing
Shaking the walls like a great ghost
A circling specter
A saint calling out to a lost god
Sing the spells that shake the dust from our souls.
Lighter, we can find Him
Uncovered, he can see us.

Sing in the stairwell
I will follow you upward
Always out of reach

The rivers run clear
The air here is exquisite
There used to be cars

The elusive voice
Why pretend this is normal?
Come with me again

Just sit and listen
The answer is in your breath
Achoooo! God bless you

I burned my fingers
Buttering roti for you
But you never eat

Tiniest mocha
Add a mountain of whipped cream
Get back to the gym!

Cowboy boots on stone
Feathers blowing across skin
Leaving scars on trails

It takes time, my dear
Smoke rises from ancient fires
But the earth turns green

From around the world
We walk down Heritage Street
Others move aside

God knows who I am
No one can know me by name
I know who I am

Our lungs are burning
In neela, saffron, and gold
The sun can't be seen

The fridge magnet girl
The Kashmiri vest salesman
No gold on this road

Café Coffee Day
A samosa and catsup
Waiting for the gang

Coronado's quest
Native blood in the canals
Ditat Dias whom?

Colonization
Coronado neighborhood
Jodha Singh's conquest

Blood, silver, and gold
Horses' hooves and gunpowder
How the West was lost

You're writing haiku
Using your Apple Notes app
And losing your soul

You tie dumala
Enemies fall like warm rain
Horse hooves thunder on

How can you judge me
With your ears pierced by fake gold
And sons clean shaven

Do you want to fight?
You want to click Like or Cry?
Comment here for rage

Pearl divers on shore
Look out over the waters
A drop falls to earth

The time in-between
Our touching and our distance
Is thick with old words

The only haiku with a title: Midnight Snack

We've broken puri
In the darkness of my car
Put the dahi in

Don't try to touch me
I can call the blood without
The word became flesh

Shinigami's charm
Rotten fruits and fresh flowers
Perfume of the dead

Lions at the gate
One on each side, sitting stone
Foes enter like ghosts

Mountain dulcimer
Cuts through the mist on the hills
Lost spirits drift home

My right hand to God
My left hand to the burnt Earth
The Mevlevis' gift

Your hands wrap around
In the strangulation dance
Your fingertips glide

The Pearl of Qatar
Shimmers throughout the bleak night
Your princely smile wins

Taming a demon
It was never so joyful
Until I caught you

The kirpan maker
And the night photographer
Record our stories

Iron, steel, and snow
The frozen will melts slowly
Patient assassin

I sit and write, "Hi"
Coups all day, comunicai
Has failed, greetings nil

Great tiger hunter
Walk with blood on the white snow
The stripes will guide you

The silence of God
The thunder of ignorance
Kirtan in between

Feed me an apple
And lock the door behind you
You're becoming me

Dust and books, gilded
Water stained and pages torn
Amritsar bookshop

My love, mi amor
Mera pyaar y your voice
Tu voz, in silence

Kites get stuck in trees
A mother rocks her baby
Wishes sail away

Cries for rain, the Earth
Demon boils the old ocean
Away to dry shores

The black ocean churns
Old timber washes ashore
White foam voice crackles

Cherry blossoms fall
Red snow melts faster than white
You'd drawn your bow well

The dancers dance on
The heels crush old bones to dust
Lungs fill with ghost songs

Warm steel mala beads
Don't cross over the life seam
Infinite prayers

The spark of a fire
The crack of a branch breaking
The forest sings dread

Soft feet crush the shells
Drops of blood embrace the sand
Warm salt water heals

Like a black forest
A creature overtakes light
Trees fall like soft hair

The darkness pushes
Into the ride's worn engine
The aged beast lurches

Pnjab's old brick roads
Falter, cracked and sunken in
Underneath lies steel

Who sold this patent?
Dreamcatcher made in China
Old ghosts get around

Moroccan tajins
Red clay passes through fingers
Tourists gawk for free

Always wear your mask
During these challenging times
Never wear a mask

Kabuki ghost screams
Audience oblivious
Rafters hold your song

I long to hear you
Sing to me from the platform
Of lies and deceit

Smoke and Birthday cake
Floating up rotting away
These days are snuffed out

Wooden angels hang
As they decorate the walls
They collect our dust

The potter's wheel spins
Empty of clay or water
His dreams lie in shards

Crack open the spine
What's inside, a spider's web
Of stories and blood

The air and the dust
Pass through Ramgharia Gate
With cracks in our feet

The numbness, the void
The blackness of cold coffee
Days at home with naught

Creativity
Wanes the moon in cold winter
Staring in judgment

Guru Gobind Singh
Your horse and blood feed the earth
Your army will rise

Guru Nanak Ji
Your children are here reading
With love in their hearts

The flies are buzzing
The hot sun bakes the new bones
A journey in vein

Give me the poor blind
Give me the dirty beggar
They're of no use there

Last name Singh: enough
Shirts on "Golden Temple" road
Blood spilled on these roads

The kulfi wala
And the destitute stray dog
Have an agreement

After 19 crimes
What's just one more broken glass
In the sea of sins

Kalimba keys chime
Metalsmith and woodworker
Make lovely music

Binary stars' song
From the VLA and back
It's a lost romance

Echoes of the rape
Girl, did you fix your make-up
Before or after

A Siva lingam
And the angular Kaaba
Claim our attention

The driftwood was there
Like a shark hunting fresh fear
Stagnant yet dreadful

Is it nap time yet
I cannot go on sleeping
Away the days pass

Liquid, help me go
On my way to better times
Wake me when we're there

I can't stop drinking
The Amrit of Guru Ji
Help me see the truth

The smell of sulfur
The weight of stones on your back
Will your basket hold?

Carved ivory dolls
Red silk with moth eaten holes
Shelves of Yurei

Winter's raging fire
Dirt, stones, and wet kindling wood
Call the demon out

Be silent, be still
Waves of creativity
Will crash on the page

Desert breeze flows hot
Cactus needles do not bend
Baked bones crack open

The thunder of bombs
Hell's fire creeps down from above
Pray Guru rakha

Crouched on the hot road
A man eats a dead dog's meat
The virus spreads on

The cold ocean swells
Sand grinds against our soft skin
We can't run from death

With burning muscles
Hold the demon at your back
He'll get inside soon

I've been collecting
Your hairs' increasing spirit
To speak a pyre spell

Sometimes, our hands touch
As you're teaching me to read
In between the lines

Grey ash falling down
Scorched black earth cradles dead leaves
Clouds gather then fade

Stay in bed, sleeping
As the sun fades away, now
The party can start

The ocean is still
My pulse quickens as you near
Waves begin to form

Stall number seven
Opposite Golden Temple
Sach weapons are sold

See the wishing star
Shield your eyes from the sharp rays
What you dream, you lose

Where should I go now
That I cannot continue
Into the rebirth

Change the behavior
Wax evolutionary
Cocoons burn away

Singing in the car
You are my Gurudwara
Words ascend to God

Ghosts try to root here
Rusted tin and rotten wood
The river takes them

By kings' and queens' blood
The lotus feeds from the mud
The kingfisher lands

Old pages of soot
Burned words and blackened scripture
Can't erase legends

Dour eventide's hold
The sun sets as old bones burn
In spite of the sea

Evacuate souls
A red, thin dust disappears
Up, into the night

Melancholy wake
An eastern, bleak ocean fades
Burial in sand

Ankle-deep oceans
An empty, wet shell crumbles
In the perfect wave

The café at night
Smoke and steam rise through the crowd
On Moroccan streets

The puzzle, the maze
Cats wind through the Medina
Seeking Muhamad

One broken promise
Topping of a mountain of lies
The summit of love

In Auntie's warm hands
Prashad rests, dripping sweet ghee
We sit cross-legged

Vampires stalk thick veins
Throbbing in the evening heat
Rising with the moon

Mother elephant
May eternal pools cool you
Your child rests with God

Two hundred and two
Haiku I wrote just for you
Please give good reviews

Oh farmer, give up
Neither your power, nor grace
The charred fields yield gold

Wooden lion toy
Your paws are splintering off
The dusty path fades

Sunbeams on buildings
Heat burns the rain into dreams
Concrete jungle grows

The horse's hooves crack
You rode here for dried-up dreams
Baked earth billows forth

In the ghosts' valley
We build high-rises on graves
Canals are their veins

The smell of crushed wheat
Slick ghee and soft hands work spells
Flames lift hungry prayers

Yellow and red tiles
The streets and drives of Pnjab
Swept into my heart

The paths of our lives
Running parallel through time
Look right and I'm there

As pyre smoke hangs low
Like a boat on the ocean
Stagnant spirit stays

Coconut oil drips
Falling between open lips
Deepam wick burns on

Land of our Gurus
Land of sants, soldiers, martyrs,
Rise above old blood

A star falls quickly
Burning away empty dreams
From love come ashes

The street dog sniffs wide
Eating from this and that dish
Catching diseases

Oni underneath
The mask is slipping away
The ugly true face

A soft body lies
About love you speak and fade
Into hate's darkness

Poodle's cute jacket
Fluffy fashion and passion
Strut that stuff, poodle

The rat finds a path
How does it go through the holes
It collapses all

Blind daruma doll
Searching in the cold half-light
Goals collecting dust

St. Francis save us
In wet markets we decay
The world can't hear us

The assassin waits
The thunder cracks over gold
Blood dyes the water

Peacock cries at night
Soul mates lost in the thick fog
The burning love dies

The forgotten Gods
Call out into the ethers
Crystals of sound fall

Your water tank burst
In the perfect calm of night
Breaking the sweet mood

Eternal cravings
Unsatisfied hunger pangs
Nothing fills your void

Why can't I sleep now
That I've lost you forever
Seems like yesterday

Sitting long enough
Haiku after haiku come
Into my lame mind

Dalang seizes us
By leather, sticks, tricks, and flames
Black and white turn grey

Food and man unite
All nations under one dish
Of love, tripe, and wine

Innocent mama
Elephant and baby burned
Away in the stream

My hollow days pass
Waiting for your poison words
Lies taste sweet but kill

Wading through oceans
Of possible syllables
Genius emerges

Our father is one
Though we are scattered like salt
Five rivers like veins

You killed your horses
Riding towards dying dreams
Who carries you now?

You removed your hair
Like a mangy dog searching
For cheap rotting flesh

You gave up your self
Begging, pathetic, and lame
Gold turned to garbage

Detroit rock city
Of passion, ruins, and chefs
Street-side and rebuilt

Hanoi fire's dawn
Chase fishermen's dreams ashore
Night lights bring the catch

Broken wings on farms
Broken dreams in fields of ash
Yet we rise as smoke

Dear rickshaw driver
We had a big tourists' meal
We'll give extra tip

Grandfather clock ticks
Grandson's mouse clicks on Tik Tok
Wood and plastic meet

She's her own poodle
I tell her to come to bed
She does what she wants

I may have no name
I may have a billion names
God knows who I am

A creature cries out
In the night air, fresh snow falls
Tears in lashes freeze

Nights in Tokyo
Sizzling meat and cute sweets
Cars and ghosts cross paths

An evening spirit
Risen from the decanter
Poured into the void

Brittle bones cracking
Breaking souls striving onward
No guards at the gates

On the slow island
Brother fights against brother
The dead trapped by time

Kings at heart bear blood
While others' chariots rust
By floods of greed's tears

The Lagos Singers
Weaving stitches of the tribes
Feet pounding the dance

Bless Eric Ripert
In Szechuan, he burned for laughs
A friend's sacrifice

Give your head to him
The master of the great hawk
Infinite rewards

As rat gives to ox
Hope and strength are born again
Year of vermin dies

Near the waterfall
Old dreams are washed up on stones
Clean, warm, and alive

Arjun's revival
Fire god finds peace in the ice
Cracks under horse hooves

A wooden doll's bones
Shifting in time on shop shelves
Dusted lungs seize breath

Infinite tears grow
Falling apart into seas
Universes bloom

A small shell holds you
As water flows constantly
The earth burns away

Corrupting the priest
In the annals of my heart
Until our last days

Why wild Rudra died;
The storms and lightning held you
But you broke your reigns

The storm and silence
Five rivers flooded with blood
Ash and smoke feed crops

In old Amritsar
British architecture rots
Gold domes hail new blood

Ice melting away
Nothing waters down the pain
The burn's eternal

The absent soul mate
The puzzle ring never solved
Gold turning to ash

The blood and the breath
The ninety-nine names of God
Bone and mud push forth

Coal miner's black soul
Flies to heaven on gold wings
Washed white by labor

Hong Kong's neon lights
Inside Chungking Mansions' husk
Taste refuge with hope

In the mood for love
Mile long escalator's view
From an endless need

Rowdy neighbors breed
Genocide of landlocked hearts
Yet genius prevails

Tattered prayer flags
Wheels turned by thunder dragons
Still, no planes have crashed

The unhinged jaw spreads
Wide expanses swallow seas
Of plastic garbage

Wooden angel wings
Floating in a sea of sin
Never get to shore

Meet me in warm pools
Of water our love is borne
As seas are teaspoons

Fall asleep by me
I can't rest without your weight
Cover me with love

Stone walls and cold grass
The castle keep, hard and wet
Standing on green fields

An old manuscript
Yellowed edges crumbling
Memories of gold

Basque's windows face in
Away from the fruitful sea
To a dying past

In Laotian soil
Bombs dream of oblivion
The people wake them

In the crystal shop
Soft people search for hard rocks
Spending food money

Through the night, I drank
Wine to unwind from the pain
I awoke in stains

I'm a saint, soldier,
Scholar, my pen is my sword
Writing words with blood

Pigeon's blood ruby
Glows near the dancers' fire light
Becomes pale at home

Stepping on dull nails
Your anklets rust in warm oil
The tabla beats you

The waxen birds melt
Into each other they run
Forming a new shape

The red bull waits there
He is ready to take her
Under the water

Our grandfather clock
Glued together yet failing
To tell time has passed

Sleep little children
Windago and Cucuy
Live only in words

Big, stagnant water
Not light nor dark, warm nor cool
Life growing from death

Fierce rain driving down
I want to taste your water
Tiger's near the pond

Things heard, yet unseen
Hell itself hides in terror
Dirt and cracking bones

Dust blows in our eyes
Cacti reaching for a drop
Monsoon's taunting ways

Shaved faces, shaved heads
A mother's tears burn her cheeks
Kes grows as armor

As days pass like dust
Traveling towards empty space
Rain and tears make mud

White tents become brown
Earth erodes as homes are built
In turn, loam and rooves

In a rotting nest
Eagle preys on broken backs
Snatching others' pride

Dust spiraling out
Blanketing boots and sandals
As men and boys play

Snow melts and blood flows
Iron and water carve stone
Five lions retreat

By pen or by gun
The politics of leaving
No one ever wins

From new life to death
Here, I saw every season
Wailing and laughter

As the tents came down
The ghosts also departed
Tied to those who lived

Blood-curdling screams
Echo through the camp at dusk
As kids play soccer

Trauma informed care
Deconstructing synergy
NGO training

In Hokkaido springs
Lava and water make love
New life bubbles forth

Fleas don't know borders
Every country is the same
A dog is a dog

Chinese made Subha
Prayer rugs dry on fences
God lives in camp too

Coyotes and djinns
Howl through the desert night air
Tent walls shudder on

An endless ocean
Words upon words, upon words
Drowning in insults

Tea bags in gravel
Sandal prints on toilet seats
Everything spilled out

Sleeping in God's palm
Worries won't dissipate yet
Nothing can go wrong

Lord Siva, I left
You stay with me despite all
What I've done to you

I am so hungry
Nobody has food I need
I can never eat

Pomegranate juice
Slowly drips into the earth
Soft dirt and tent spikes

Randomly, men walk
Searching in and out of tents
They find no answers

Lights begin dimming
Lost souls fly towards new abodes
Call of emptiness

In the desert air
Heat, dust, rain, and tears mingle
Bound by transience

As filth encroaches
People cower under beds
Beds made of storm cells

Heat's in the valley
Ghosts are in the riverbed
Hope of rain abates

Black curtains come down
As the drama dissipates
The actors' death march

The wailing woman
Of Doña Ana, we think
And the tears reach down

Under torn canvas
Scraps of camp coated in dust
Grass sprouts through the floor

Bird in the death throes
We drink tea and watch it fade
Oceans of black tea

Fire above the earth
And ice below the cave walls
The ancient Gods' bed

Master of Data
Open to interruption
Open heart, closed case

Weeping in the dirt
La Llorona of Fort Bliss
Fled Panjshir River

Light fixtures swaying
Fixed figures vacillating
Between bright and dim

Hot springs, take my tears
Like snow melting into pools
So my sorrows thin

Tasting free honey
With Bismillah on our lips
Our hands are empty

Gentle ghost of lights
Floating through the old circuits
Fading in and out

Kintsugi soul broke
Into fine dust and gold tears
Weeping made it whole

One meter stretch tea
Spices boiling with passion
Cooling in still air

Jugnu, light my way
Through the shadows of tall ghosts
Take me home with you

With black eyes staring
And cold hands scratching stone walls
The spirit entered

I found you sleeping
In the middle of the night
You reached for my hand

By coconut leaves
Kettuvallam drifts eschew
A bather looks on

Under Banyan trees
I slept for a million years
My bones became roots

Tearing down houses
The dust of dead dreams rises
Infecting our lungs

Mandatory fun
A vacation from my life
No sun on the beach

Turning back and forth
We're addicted to heartbreak
And we run from love

Growing through trauma
We all left our shells behind
Now comes the real pain

The most aural screams
Come from a place of silence
Black ink on white cloth

The vendors oven
Feeds the streets and families
Creation and waste

As storms die away
Black clouds become grey specters
Love becomes cobwebs

Lapis dealer's shop
Stones are behind glass borders
In Afghanistan

Tea stains in the cup
The new kettle's frayed wires
Guests in camp, zero

Doomed attan dancers
The scorpion and lion
Each defending home

I didn't go home
From tears to pools to oceans
I swam from my home

I'm just a small girl
I want my mom to be strong
She should be stronger

Six syllable lines
And four-part sentences, see!
Curse me every time!

As the end draws near
The resources become scarce
Blinking cursor's curse

As youth escapes us
We gain the tools to survive
The traumas of youth

Hulusi's droning
Echoes through the stone ally
The bao maker sways

The rickshaw's driver
Nandini and calf muscles
Burn to the temple

On the Dreamtime's shores
The songlines are as our veins
Mapping our way home

Soft buns full of meat
Bamboo baskets catching steam
My sweet dumpling dreams

The shaking hand bleeds
Scratching through tranquil forests
Unearthing dark truths

As cancer shapes cells
So your words blacken my soul
We'll all be dead soon

In drawn arrow's gaze
Through wind, the artery called
There was no escape

On bookshelves and desks
Sit tchotchkes and real treasures
Drawing the same dust

Panjshir jeweler
Taliban stole his emeralds
And burned down his house

In the Guru's path
We stumble over laughter
Tears too are prashad

Stone lions keep guard
One paw on village offspring
One paw on the world

Prayer wheels can't rust
We cry perpetually
Not hearing answers

In turn, blood and dirt
From birth to the universe
Stars pulse through our veins

One more haiku to write
Like the chip placed into the perfect vase
Only God is perfect

Afterword

Now you know haiku
Thank you for reading my book
Have a lovely day

I sincerely thank you for reading my book of 365 haiku poems. I wrote my first haiku poem in the 7th grade a part of a larger poetry project. It is included in this volume as haiku number two. Since that time, I have been inspired to write more haiku for the Phoenix Matsuri, and have been honored to win several contests. The thing I love about haiku is the necessity for supreme potency of creativity inside extreme restraint. In just three lines, 17 syllables, the author must create an entire narrative, paint a complete picture, and enrapture the reader in an immersive scene. It's an incredible challenge, one that I have strived to achieve within these pages to varying degrees of success. The subject matter in this tome has come from many places such as my participation in a local taiko dojo, observation of everyday life, world travel, the honored travels of Anthony Bourdain, heartbreak and life lessons learned, and most recently, my time employed in an Afghan evacuee camp in the middle of the New Mexico desert. My haiku are meant to appeal to everyone despite their knowledge about my personal goings on; although, if you know these specific inspirations, you will no doubt have a different interpretation of the pieces. Final note: haiku number 311 appears to include an error, but it is perfectly as I wish it to be.

Again, my most genuine appreciation for you, my audience.

Made in the USA
Coppell, TX
10 February 2022